THE PRODIGAL FATHER

By:

Lawrence O. Olayele

To order additional copies of this book, contact:
Proisle Publishing Services LLC
1177 6th Ave 5th Floor
New York, NY 10036, USA
Phone: (+1 347-922-3779)
info@proislepublishing.com

PROISLE PUBLISHING

Table of Contents

Dedication

This book is appreciatively dedicated to the glory of my Lord Jesus Christ, whose love and grace I have enjoyed in every area of my life.

Also, to my darling wife, Victoria, whose love for me for more than four decades has never waned. Who can find a virtuous woman? I did by God's grace.

To my beloved children and grandchildren, whose fellowship we cherish more than the world. We will never be lonely.

Preface

About five years ago, I went to Nigeria during the summer. As my custom, I tried as much as I could to stop for a day or two in most of the major cities where my family or friends live. On this particular trip, I stayed with one of my brothers at Ile-Ife, a city in the South West for two days. On the first morning during their devotion, my brother, who is a pastor, asked me to share the Word of God with the family. I can't remember what passage of the Bible we read, but I decided to explain to them by the Spirit of God the grace of God in my life. Sharing the reckless life I lived as a teenager and young adult was a surprise to them. His four teenage children could not believe the vile person their most respected uncle (me) was while growing up. They thought I had always been a good and godly person. I concluded it is the grace of God that justified the ungodly.

Interestingly, some of them know, and have heard from some of my old, unconverted friends who still scratch their heads as to how God could justify someone like me, considering our past.

The use of "Prodigal Father" as the title, is not in contrast to the parable of the Prodigal Son in the book of Luke 15: 11-32 as most Christians are familiar with. The emphasis of the title is on the word "Prodigal" meaning one who spends his resources freely, recklessly, lavishly, extravagantly, profusely, and without any restraint.

The theme of this book is to expose the extravagant love of God to humanity. The book may provide a fresh revelation of the love the Father has for us, His children. It will also make the Gospel more inviting to the unbelieving world with the message of salvation in a way that the concept of "for God so loved the world" will become more meaningful to them.

Introduction

This book is set forth in childlike dependence on the power of the Holy Spirit to explain the love of God that provides salvation for His people in a simple form than most people have ever explained or heard. My goal is to further expose to intellectuals and unlearned what the death, burial, and resurrection of Jesus Christ have done for us; not what religion or theologians can do for us.

Humans, because of our pride, still want to believe there must be something in us that is good; good enough to pay at least part of our sin debt. Good enough to be a part of our redemption or justification so that we can please God, but God declares in Romans 3:10: "There is none righteous, No, not one." Isaiah 64:6 says, "All our righteousness are filthy rags." Therefore, the Lord Jesus Christ did not come into the world expecting to find goodness or righteousness in anyone, but to give it to as many people who dare to believe their own goodness or righteousness does not cut it. He came to justify the ungodly. A lawyer goes to court to plead the case of an innocent man so that he can be set free from being falsely accused. In effect, He wants to justify the innocent, not protect the guilty. Jesus Christ in contract come to protect the guilty, the ungodly.

Unfortunately, many ungodly people don't know the gravity of their depravity. They live on the planet rich with all the blessings of God's abundant provision of air, water, and minerals only to call them "chance." That can only be the height of ignorance of ungodliness and an insult to God. However, even in their blindness, He came to justify them. Like my own pathetic state when I was a kid, even when I was raised in the church, I enjoyed going to church every Sunday, sang in the choir, participated in all Sunday school activities, and annual harvest entertainment. I started thinking if God would justify the ungodly, I was more qualified than the ungodly, only to find out my self-righteousness was a delusion. God's salvation is for the ungodly people who have no preparation for it. In Matthew 9:13, Jesus says He did not come to call the righteous even when He already knew there were none. I set up each chapter in a way to bring forth the love of God in various ways that can lead anybody to the saving knowledge of Jesus Christ. I deliberately deviate from the traditional way of witnessing the "salvation" message. To bring forth the grace of God in this way had been in my mind for a long time considering the way the Lord drew me to Himself. When I started hearing messages on the grace of God, it resonated in my spirit right away, more than any message on salvation and godly living I had ever heard. The grace of Jesus Christ, our righteousness, God's highest gift to humanity, should awaken our deepest gratitude.

When I consider the many ways the Lord opened my eyes to His love and grace, I don't have any other way to describe it than to call Him the Prodigal Father.

God's reckless grace is our greatest hope. 2 Corinthians 5:21 says, "For He (God) made Him (Jesus) who knew no sin to be sin for us, that we might become the righteousness of God in Him."

I therefore plead with the readers of this book not to receive the love and grace of this Father in vain.

Chapter 1

The Lavish Love of the Father in Salvation

An average human being is always concerned about what happens to him or her when death comes. Is death the end of everything? Even Job wanted to know about this. In Job 19:14, Job asked, "If a man dies, shall he live again?" Thousands of years later after so many generations must have discussed or debated on this issue, a religious leader came to Jesus to ask a related question (John 3:1-21). In Nicodemus' case, he knew there was life after death, but being "born again" into a relationship with his maker was his concern.

A person's future with regards to where he or she will spend eternal life should be of paramount concern. God, because of His love for us, did not leave us without an answer. In the passage above, Jesus made the process of being born again clear. In John 11:25-26, Jesus also said, "I am the resurrection and the life. He who believes in me, though he may die, he shall live. And whoever lives and believes in me shall never die."

When a person accepts Jesus Christ us Savior and Lord, the person is born again, or is saved (John 3:3, Romans 10:9). When God created the earth, He gave man the dominion over all His creation (Genesis 1:26). The devil came to tempt Eve to eat of the forbidden fruit of the tree that God had earlier commanded Adam not to eat. By this act of disobedience, Adam put the earth and all mankind whom he represented under the dominion of Satan. This led mankind to a spiritual death, not to talk of physical death, of which everyone is familiar. Because of the extravagant love of God for man, He decided to provide or remedy this in His Son, the second person of the triune Godhead, the Lord Jesus Christ. God wanted to put man back to his original state of intimate relationship He had with man at the beginning.

The love of God in doing this caused Jesus Christ His separation from God on the cross leading to His death, served our term in hell, but resurrected and presented himself an acceptable sacrifice to God. His resurrection serves as the receipt that our sins have been paid in full. Choosing to receive Jesus Christ as your Savior and Lord is the most important decision anyone will ever make in life because it is the one thing that is needed to enjoy all the Father has provided. Romans 10:9-10 says, "That if you confess with your mouth the Lord Jesus and believe in your heart that God has raised Him from the dead, you will be saved. For with the heart one believes unto righteousness, and with the mouth confession is made unto salvation."

By His grace, God has already provided salvation through His extravagant love. There is nothing for you to do other than to believe and receive the gift. The Bible says all that is required of you is to confess with your mouth and believe in your heart. Each time I explain this is all that is needed for salvation, some religious friends want to say people need more. They say sinners must confess their sins in addition to believing to be truly saved. Think about it: how many sins will an unbeliever remember to confess? The sins he committed today, or last week, or last year, or all the sins he has ever committed? What about the sins he has forgotten about, or the sins he never counted as important, though grievous in the sight of God? The sin of unbelief is what the world will be judged. The Lord only wants an unbeliever to accept Jesus Christ as the Savior, the substitute for our sin. God does not require or ask an unbeliever to start to recount or confess his sin actions as if He never knew them. I am not saying God will be angry at a sinner who decides to confess his sins in addition to confessing Jesus as the Savior, but the confession of sins is not required, and that does not lead to salvation.

Let us look at a passage of the scripture that captures what I have been trying to explain. After Jesus had fed about five thousand men, not counting children and women by the Sea of Tiberias, He went to the other side of the sea. Some of the people who participated in the previous day feasting on the miracle of feeding of over five thousand men (with five loaves of barley and two small fish) came looking for Jesus again. The conversation between them according to John 6:26-29 goes like this:

> "Most assuredly, I say to you, you seek Me, not because you saw the signs, but because you ate of the loaves and were filled. Do not labor for the food which perishes, but for the food which endures to everlasting life, which the Son of Man will give you because God the Father has set His seal on Him."

Then they said to Him, "What shall we do, that we may work the works of God?" Jesus answered and said to them, "This is the work of God, that you believe in Him whom He sent."

People during the days of Jesus Christ wanted to do some work for their salvation, like people of today who want to add a little more to believing the only acceptable sacrifice that God has richly provided in Jesus Christ. Maybe they were more interested in performing miracles like Jesus Christ instead of receiving the life of God. The response of Jesus was simple: "Believe in Him whom He sent." It is interesting that Jesus did not ask them to start to confess their sins, but only believe in Him as the solution to their spiritual and physical needs. If you truly want to know this Father God with all these provisions, He will reveal Himself to you as He did to Simon Peter in Matthew 16:17. Jesus wanted to find out from His disciples who the people thought He was. After the disciples rambled about this question for some time, Jesus asked the same question from them.

"Who do you say that I am?"

Peter answered, "You are the Christ, the Son of the living God."

To this answer, Jesus responded, "Blessed are you, Simon Bar Jonah, for flesh and blood has not revealed this to you, but my Father who is in heaven."

At times I wonder how I came to understand the good news that set a sinner like me free while others don't. It is the Father who reveals Himself to all who hear about His grace through the Holy Spirit that Jesus Christ is the Savior of the world.

In addition to granting salvation to all who believe in Him, Jesus also made it clear, "whosoever comes to Him, He will by no means cast out" (John 6:37). Jesus does not only save, He keeps all that comes to Him to the end.

Verses 39-40 reveal more of the love of the Father for us:

> This is the will of the Father who sent Me, that of all He has given Me, I should lose nothing, but should raise it up at the last day, and this is the will of Him who sent Me, that everyone who sees the Son and believes in Him may have everlasting life; and I will raise him up at the last day.

What a loving Father! He made a promise that anyone who comes to Him is secured and will not be lost. He will not lose anyone because He is a great, powerful, and merciful God. Believe this and come to the rest He alone can provide.

No one understands and appreciates the prodigal love of the Father in salvation like King David. In Psalm 8:3, David proclaims, "When I consider your heavens, the work of your fingers, the moon and the stars which you have ordained. What is man that you are mindful of him. And the son of man that you visit (give attention, or care for) him?"

It can only be a prodigal Father who can make such a provision for His creation at a sweep.

Salvation, to many believers and churchgoers is only about getting saved and missing hell when they die. This is a good beginning, but that is just the beginning of the heart of God. Salvation is total forgiveness of our sin—past, present, and future. It also means healing, protection, provision, prosperity, and general wellbeing!

Luke 15:1 reveals those who came to hear Jesus were sinners and tax collectors; the colleagues and friends of Matthew. Jesus began this message about repentance by talking about a man with 100 sheep. In the similar account in the book of Matthew, the Lord actually began by asking His listeners:

What do you think? If a man owns a hundred sheep, and one of them wanders away, will he not leave the ninety-nine on the hills and go to look for the one that wandered off? And if he finds it, truly I tell you, he is happier about that one sheep than about the ninety-nine that did not wander off.

In our normal human life, nobody leaves ninety-nine sheep in search of one missing sheep. This can only be a kind of love that is beyond comprehension: the love of the Father. Here, Jesus starts to show the heart of the father toward sinners. Don't forget, His listeners are the sinners and tax collectors, the cheats of society. These were people who betrayed their country by collecting taxes for the Roman government and then pocketed part of it.

This was what Zaccheus referred to when he said, in Luke 19:86, "If I have taken anything from anyone by false accusation, I restore fourfold." These were the people to whom Jesus explained the heart of His father. In this parable, Jesus made it clear how dear one lost sinner is to the Father. He searches as long as it takes until he finds Him. The emphasis here is not the lost sheep but the "man." Unfortunately, our preaching has always been about the word "repent" here, but the sheep did not repent, but were sought and found by the owner. The love (grace) of the Father keeps searching and looking for the lost souls.

Jesus' teaching was attractive to sinners. Many of the messages in churches today are full of intellectualism, things that are irrelevant to average people in understanding the love of God. Does a sinner care about hell? Does a sinner understand what hell is or represents? I still remember when I was in the world without Jesus, Christians who used hell to "scare" me did not make sense to me. I am not saying there is no hell; the Bible talks about it and I believe it as a place for the devil, demons, and all who fail to believe in Jesus Christ as the only Savior of the world. What a sinner would gravitate to is the lavish love a Father who does not want anyone to perish, but have eternal life. They need to know the love of a man who would leave ninety-nine sheep and go searching for a lost one. A Father who will rejoice over one sheep rather than the other ninety-nine. If a sinner comes to church because he is afraid of going to hell, he will meet many situations in his "church walk" that will drive him out of the church back to the world. However, if a sinner comes to the kingdom because he understands the extravagant love of the Father, he or she will love and appreciate the Father in every circumstance of life and would not want to go back to the world of judgment and condemnation.

The Prodigal Son (Luke 15:11-32): Some even call this parable "The Parable of the Two Lost Sons."

"My inheritance now!" is a sign of deep disrespect and dishonor, and a wish that the father dies statement. He wants his father's things, not the father in an intensely patriarchal society in which great honor and respect to one's parents were paramount. A traditional Middle Eastern family would have driven the son out with nothing, but his father simply divided his property (*bios* - life in Greek). If the man had invested in real estate, to give the son his own third (as was the custom for the younger son), he would have had to sell his property. The son, in asking his father to tear his life apart because of him, accounts to the height of selfishness and dishonor to the father. This would have been hurtful, shameful, and degrading to his father, but he consented. How many times have we rejected the love of God, put Him in shame in private as well as in public? How many times we ridiculed His love and patience for us? I remember as a sinner, I would make fun of the believers who witnessed to me by asking them questions like: "Where is this God you are talking about?" "Where is heaven or hell?" "Who tells you that the Bible is real?" This attitude did not diminish the love of God for a sinner like me. He kept searching for me like the man with one lost sheep out of 100.

Two sons, one "bad" by convectional standard and one "good," yet both are alienated from the father. No one is just, the Father still searches for His lost children today. "For all have sinned and fall short of the glory of God" (Romans 3:23).

It is incomprehensive for the self-righteous elder brother to imagine how quickly his father would forgive his brother. They both want the father's goods rather than the father himself. Each wants to get to the position of self-righteousness. One did so by being "bad" and the other by being "good," being obedient without any sin. Both were alienated from the father's heart, both were lost, but the grace and love of the father brought them both back to him. In the practical sense of it, neither son loves the father for himself. They used the father for their own self-centeredness rather than loving, enjoying, and serving the father for his sake. What is your motive in the family?

Someone once said one way to avoid Jesus as Savior is to keep all moral laws. If you do that, then you have "rights" before God. Do you think your good moral life is a ticket to heaven when you die, and you don't need a Savior to grant you His free gift of grace and righteousness?

If you have not renewed your mind with the Word of God, as an older generation of Christian, one can from time to time slide into the spirit of the elder brother. This manifests by condemning, being joyless, angry, and condescending anytime you see the newer crops of Christians in the way they sing, dress, and rejoice in the Lord. If you think goodness and decency is the way to merit a good life from God, you will be eaten up with anger, and you will always feel like God is cheating you. You will always ask why the other person is being blessed more than you. Elder brothers always have a feeling of superiority based on being hardworking, moral, savvy, and extremely smart.

Sin is not just breaking the rules or laws of God; it is putting yourself in the place or before God as Savior and Lord. The gospel of Jesus is not religion or irreligion, morality or immorality, moralism or relativism, conservatism or liberalism, republican or democrat. The prerequisite to receiving the grace of God is to know you need it. You need a Savior and you are ready to believe Him.

It is not recited repentance that causes the Father's love. I am sure some believers will disagree with this statement because of what we have always believed about the word "repentance." Reading through the story again, we can see the son has not even gotten have way through the planned repentant speech when his father interrupted him. The Father's love and acceptance is absolutely free. Nothing, not even abject contrition, merits the favor of God. Each time I remember walking away from the love of God as a child, no word like, "I am sorry," or, "I repent" is ever enough to express how I felt. Each time my mind strays to my inadequacy of the word to use, I catch myself, and remind myself that no even contrition merits the love, grace, and forgiveness of God.

I once heard a pastor say when Jesus went to the house of Zaccheus in Luke 19:1, he wouldn't have been saved until he confessed his sins to Jesus. Let us take a look at what transpired between Jesus and Zaccheus in this passage. In verse 5, the Bible says, Jesus looked up, saw and said, "Zaccheus, make haste and come down, for today I must stay in your house." All of these are deliberate actions of calling a sinner to the love of the father. Even though Zaccheus started to recount what he did, like the prodigal son trying to buy back his father's forgiveness and a place in the family, Jesus was not impressed with that. That was not the reason why He was there. He was there to extend the heart of the Father to the world. Jesus did not wait for him to recount all his good work. What Jesus came to do is clear in verses 9-10. This is a message of the love and grace of God.

It shows even the most religious and moral people need the initiation of grace from our Heavenly Father. Actually, the more religious a person is, the more difficult it is for him to see the love of the Father. A religious person would want to prove he has been good, and that his work should count for something.

As believers, we should always remember we would have never known the Lord if He hadn't sought us. His love always brings us to the end of ourselves. His love brings us to repentance that is genuine and lasting.

In the other two parables of the lost sheep and lost coin, many people almost automatically know the owner should be the one looking for the lost material. However, in the case of the prodigal son, no one expects the father to be the one looking out for his son. I believe this is why Jesus asked His listeners in Matthew 18:12, "What do you think?" Can you imagine this situation? Does this sound right to you? Is this situation normal? Is there a respectable father who could tolerate this behavior? How can God in His power and majesty decide to make Himself a sacrifice for His disobedient and lost creation when He has the power to wipe us off and create a new set of human being? Couldn't the elder brother have pleaded with his father to even be more generous to his lost brother for coming back home to the family?

Forgiveness always comes at a cost to the one granting it. The younger brother's restoration was free to him, but it came at enormous cost to the elder brother. In the natural, the father could not reinstate him except at the expense of the older brother. However, in our case, we don't have an elder brother who has taken the larger part of the inheritance. The Father we have possesses the whole world. No elder brother to take 2/3 of our father's possessions; our inheritance is always whole, not 1/3. Unlike our elder brother, the story's elder brother knew bringing back his brother would mean a lot of losses to him. He will have to share the remaining 2/3 to that belongs to him with his brother. "My son, everything I have is yours." This is true, according to their tradition. In our limited understanding of their culture, we try to spiritualize this statement. He was afraid he would have to share what is left in the house. As it cost his elder brother something, like it cost Jesus Christ, our elder brother, his life. The elder brother we have is willing to look out for us. Our true elder brother paid our debt on the cross—no, He overpaid our debt. God did not only forget our sins, but forgave and forgot them because they have been fully paid for. He was stripped naked of His robe and dignity so that we could be clothed with dignity and honor (Philippians 2:6-8). Knowing He did this for us will transform us from the inside out. His selfless love destroys the mistrust in our hearts toward God.

John Newton's friend, the poet, William Cowper, summaries it like this:

"To see the law by Christ fulfilled,

And hear his pardoning voice,

Changes a slave into a child

And duty into choice."

It is the prodigal love of the Father that can forgive a wayward son, bring him in, restore him to his position in the family, and robe him back with the robe of righteousness. In a culture where meat was reserved for special occasions like my own society where I grew up, feasting with the most expensive meat is extravagant for a wayward child. That is exactly what Jesus did for us. God's love pardons the vilest sinners.

Timothy Keller says, "By putting a flawed elder brother in the story, Jesus is inviting us to imagine and yearn for a true one." Our elder brother did not go out of His comfort zone in search of us, but was also willing to pay with His own life for all that we have lost. He does not begrudge our being in the party but invites us back to the great party. The only way for the Heavenly Father to bring us back to the family is at the expense of our true elder brother.

Chapter 2

The Lavish Love of the Father in Forgiveness

The Father knows fallen man can't keep His law perfectly, and He looked for a way to help us understand this simple truth. Unfortunately, we got stuck to the desire to try to keep the law as our way of pleasing God.

Satan planted the seed of sin in the hearts of Adam and Eve in the Garden of Eden when Eve was deceived to disobey God. Since then, sin came to the world and death, both spiritual and physical, came later. There might be some people who argue this and feel since they are morally good, they are not sinners. I have nothing for such people in this chapter. Luke 1:53 is a summary of God's word for such people: "He both filled the hungry with good things, and the rich (self-righteous ones) He sent empty away." To those of us who believe on the account of Adam, the first Adam, you have been a partaker of his sinful nature, God says, "I will forgive their iniquity and I will remember their sin no more."

Jeremiah 31: 31-34:

> "Behold, the days are coming," says the Lord, "when I will make a new covenant with the house of Israel and with the house of Judah-not according to the covenant that I made with their fathers in the day that I took them by the hand to lead them out of the land of Egypt, My covenant which they broke, though I was a husband to them," says the Lord. "But this is the covenant that I will make with the house of Israel after those days," says the Lord: "I will put My law in their hearts; and I will be their God, and they shall be My people. No more shall every man teach his neighbor, and

every man his brother, saying, 'Know the Lord,' for they all shall know Me, from the least of them to the greatest of them," says the Lord. "For I will forgive their iniquity, and their sin I will remember no more."

Only the love of a Prodigal Father can be so deep. The house of Israel and Judah could not keep the law, the first covenant like all of us couldn't, He devised another means to rescue us. Our part in this new covenant is to trust and believe Him. Jesus sowed His life and He wants us to reap His righteousness! As if this promise is not enough, our Father God confirmed it again in Isaiah 54:10: "For the mountain shall depart and the hills be removed, But My kindness shall not depart from you, nor shall My covenant of peace be removed,' says the Lord, who has mercy on you."

Don't draw a timeline of God's forgiveness of your sins. This passage says we have been forgiven of all our trespasses. Unfortunately, some Christians believe the sins they have been forgiven of are from the day they were born until they became Christians and from then on, they have to be extra careful so that they don't lose their salvation. This leads such believers again to think they must work for their salvation. The Bible says by Jesus' one sacrifice on the cross, all our sins are forgiven. Hebrews 7:27 says our High Priest, Jesus Christ, offered himself a complete, perfect, and acceptable sacrifice once and for all unlike the high priests of the Old Testament or covenant that had to repeat the sacrifices yearly. Jesus does not have to be crucified again for our sins of today or those of tomorrow. When He died over two thousand years ago, all of our sins were far, far in the future. It can only be a prodigal father who will, ahead of time and age, forgive sins that have not even been committed. This may sound like giving a license for people to sin, but not if one appreciates the love, the extravagant love a Father who knows the end of everyone even from the beginning.

In Luke 7:36-50, a Pharisee named Simon invited Jesus to his house. As Jesus was seated, a woman in the city came. The Bible calls her a sinner, which most likely meant she was a prostitute. She stood at Jesus' feet weeping and washing His feet with her tears and wiping them with her hair. She kissed his feet and anointed them with a costly oil of alabaster she brought with her. She probably had encountered Jesus Christ before only to show up again in appreciation for her sins that have been forgiven. But when Simon saw this, he said in his mind, "This man, if he were a prophet, would know who and what manner of woman this is who is touching him, for she is a sinner." Even though Simon did not speak out loud, but Jesus knew his thinking.

Jesus posed this question to Simon. "There was a certain creditor who had two debtors. One owed five hundred denarii, and the other fifty and when they had nothing with which to repay, he freely forgave them both. Tell me, therefore which of them will love him more?"

Simon answered, "I suppose the one whom he forgave more."

Jesus said to him, "You have rightly judged."

The woman loved Jesus much because she knew she was forgiven much. Many people don't know they have been forgiven much. Every one of us has been forgiven much. As a born-again believer, the root cause of sin has been removed. God's forgiveness is not installmental. If you believe His forgiveness for you is on installment basis, then you will love only when you feel you are forgiven.

If you believe His forgiveness is much, you will love much. If you believe your sins have been fully dealt with and forgiveness at the cross, you will have much confidence to enjoy the Lord's presence at all times. You will not allow the spirit of condemnation to ruin your relationship with your Heavenly Father. You will have the boldness to come to the throne of Grace each time there is a need in your life. You will, like the woman in Simon's house, be free to worship Him without intimidation from the world. You will not be in the circle of insecurity only hopping good might happen to you instead of a constant expectation of goodness from your prodigal Father. The only time you judge right in the kingdom of God is when you know all your sins have been forgiven. Your relationship with others will be great because it will be easy for you to instantly forgive others, as the Lord desires of us.

Sin cannot take root in a person who is full of consciousness that Jesus loves him. Such a person becomes the righteousness of God in Christ Jesus. The prodigal love of the Father will cast off all fear.

Romance 8:1: "Therefore there is now no condemnation for those who are in Christ Jesus." There is now no condemnation to those in Christ Jesus because of the extravagant love of the Father. Unfortunately, not many believers walk in this understanding. Forgiveness of sins is based on His grace, the unmerited favor of God. We have access to this grace by faith. If you take away the forgiveness of sins from the gospel, then it is no longer good news.

Jeremiah 31:34: "I will forgive their iniquity, and I will remember their sin no more." This means *never again* will He remember our sin. The Lord, the prodigal father, is the one saying, "I will forgive and blot out" all our sin. Sometimes I think the reason why we do not appreciate the gravity of sin is because we have the tendency to categorize them. If, for example, I have not killed anyone, or committed adultery, or stolen anybody's property, then I might feel I am okay before

God. If He forgives all my sins, that is fine because they are not big anyway. They should be easy for Him to overlook and forgive. However, if I have committed adultery and killed someone before, the mention of forgiveness will become more significant to me. Unfortunately, the Lord does not group sins as we do. He says every unrighteousness is sin. If you have not accepted the only acceptable righteousness, which is of Jesus Christ, you are a sinner. Our unbelief is sin. Adam's disobedience to a simple command led human beings to the path of separation from our creator and brought sin and death to man. When our children were all with us in their tender years, I used to tell them about my concern that because they have not encountered so much of the life of sin, they might not appreciate the love and holiness of God as I do. Basing our righteousness on the act of sin as a justification for our holiness or the lack of it will not allow us the full recognition of the forgiveness of sin the father has granted us.

"For God so loved the world…"

Many people do not understand this kind of love. Before Jesus gave Himself as the Lamb of God who took away the sin of the world, He tried to explain this love in many parables and teachings. Unfortunately, not many people of His time understood His message. Even now, over two thousand years after He lived among men, died, resurrected, and ascended to heaven, many people still can't comprehend the extravagant, prodigal love of His Father. Many who are already born again, or saved or believe in Him still teach others about self-righteousness and self-effort other than the love of the Father that brings man to repentance and the saving knowledge of God. On our own we can't do anything to merit the salvation and righteousness that is required by God. I usually joke with a dear friend of mine whenever we discuss the grace of God in our lives. We joke (though not a laughing matter) how we wouldn't have qualified if we had to pay for our salvation considering our poor backgrounds. We say the Western world would have bought everything before anybody in Africa knew about it. Not stopping there, we concluded people in the cities would have bought the little left for Africa even before people like us that live all our lives in the interior villages know anything about it. How miserable our lives would have been! Yet, thanks be to this prodigal Father who not only provides the grace to receive free salvation and righteousness, but also provides the grace to receive it. He did not provide a city of refuge without the way to enter its gate. In the story of the Good Samaritan, in Luke 10:34, when he, the "Prodigal Father" who I will depict as the Good Samaritan saw the traveler (a certain man, that is, you or me) lying wounded and half dead the Good Samaritan, did not ask him to rise up and come to him. He went to him. Jesus came to us in this wretched world and ministered the heart of His father to us. Allow me to retell this story again, each time I read it, I can't help but shout, "Praise the Lord" for His prodigal love for me.

In Luke 10:25, a lawyer stood up to test Jesus Christ about what to do to inherit eternal life.

"And behold, a certain lawyer stood up and tested Him, saying, "Teacher, what shall I do to inherit eternal life?" He said to him, "What is written in the law?" "What is your reading of it?"

Man wants to do something to earn his salvation. Pride of man will never allow him to receive and believe. Jesus directed him to the law to prove to him that no one can fulfill all that is written in it to the satisfaction of God. Nonetheless, the lawyer quoted what the law says. Even now that we are empowered by the spirit of God dwelling in us, no one can boast that he or she can "Love the Lord your God with all your heart, with all your soul and with all your strength, and with all your mind, and your neighbor as yourself." Who can love Him with all his soul, mind, and energy? No one. Nonetheless, Jesus commended him for quoting this passage correctly. He wanted to further prove he already understood the heart of Jesus, so He went ahead to ask, "Who is my neighbor?"

Jesus then used the opportunity again to explain the prodigal love of His father. A certain man (humanity) went from daily fellowshipping with his father God as in the Garden of Eden to a broken relationship and into the world of Satan (Jerusalem to Jericho). He fell among thieves of the world.

It appears as if the world is being filled with more robbers than any other time in human history. Look at every continent of the world today. It is one form of robbery or the other. If there is no AIDS, Ebola, Covid-19, there is an unending war all around the world. If none of these appears in your zone, there are natural disasters that come upon the earth unexpectedly. What about sudden deaths of loved ones or sudden disappearance of airplanes with hundreds of souls without a trace? The list goes on and on. Ask the people who have been struck by any of these calamities of this world. They will tell you that they are dead or half dead in the way they feel about the world already.

Verse 31: "Now by chance…" It is by chance that anyone could heal our wounds and if they do, it can't last. A priest, a prophet, or a close relative can't heal our wounds. They don't have the compassion or the means to make you whole. Yet, when Jesus (the certain Samaritan) came, He had compassion on the half-dead man. He went to him, He bandaged his wounds, He poured oil and wine on the wounds, and set him on his own animal. At this point, he had to be walking behind or beside the animal because the wounded man took his seat. He took him to an inn and paid for his care. As if this was not enough, he promised, "Take care of him, and whatever more you spend, when I come again, I will repay you." The Lord says if all He has done is not enough, He will come back again to pay even more. Tell me if this is prodigal or not. If you accidentally come across a half-dead person on the road, will you take him to the hospital and pay for the initial cares with the promise of coming back to make more payment for a situation you did not cause? I won't, but the Prodigal Father did. In Matthew 9:36, the Bible records when He saw the multitudes, He was moved with compassion for them because they were weary or harassed by their problems and scattered like sheep with no shepherd. Psalm 78:38 says, "But He being full of compassion, forgave their iniquity." souls and a life without Christ. Imagine a half-dead man on a donkey. He was likely no longer aware of his environment. He might not be able to lift his hands or legs. He probably was half-naked also. Yet, the Good Samaritan set him on his donkey, took him to an Inn for more attention, and providing a lifetime of care. The prodigal father did not just save us from sins and from spiritual death; He poured the oil of His Spirit on us. He quickened us from being half-dead from the attacks of the enemy of our soul. In the same way, Jesus made provision for us in our journey to a life of eternity with Him and gave us His position high in the heavens above principalities and power. He also promised He is coming back again. John 14:3: "And if I go and prepare a place for you, I will come again and receive you to myself; that where I am, there you may be also." Once we know the love of God for us, we become the object of His care; then we can start to enjoy all His provision.

I once heard a Christian friend lamenting this Christian walk is difficult. I understand the challenges in the way a believer shouldn't love the things of the world. I know there are many worldly short cuts that lead to nowhere. As Christians, we want to live like the saints we are called, but it looks as if the demand on our flesh is too great. At a time when you feel like this, you need to ask the question, "Who am I?" Are you a pig trying to live like a sheep? Of course that will require a lot of effort. Understanding our identity is one sure way of enjoying your Christian walk. No one can consistently behave in a way that is inconsistent with the way he thinks of himself or herself and still be at peace. Knowledge of who we are is an important truth that can set us on the right path for staying focused in our Christian walk. If you believe you are nothing but a pig, nothing can prevent you from going back to the mud at every available opportunity. Our identity in Christ is the truth that can set us free to live for the one that saved us.

A proper understanding of our identity in Christ is a sufficient motivation to have a totally different attitude toward sin. If you understand you are no longer a pig, you will not want to wallow in a mud. Actually, you will want to stay away from mud. I have never seen a sheep wallowing in a mud before. As a saint, you go on the offense against sin because you know who you are. As a believer, a sinful lifestyle contradicts my nature. As a Christian, I do not allow the affairs of this world to bog me down to make my walk with Christ difficult. If "this way" sounds difficult, I need to check my identity. Am I a pig with the wrong identity? Carrying a different identity from who you are is the reason why Jesus told his hearers in John11:28, "Come to me, all you who labored and are heavy laden, and I will give you rest. Take my yoke upon you, and learn from me, for I am gentle and lowly in heart, and you will find rest for your souls. For my yoke is easy and my burden is light." His blood has purchased a new identity for me. My part is to believe that and walk in that consciousness always. Do I imply a simple life without trials and challenges? I pray you do not read that from my writing.

His lavish love leads me from condemnation. Many Christians go through the motivation – condemnation – redemption cycle. When they hear a "nice" sermon, they think a wide gap between them and God has been shortened. When they do anything unchristian, they feel condemned and go to church to rededicate their lives, confessing their spiritual slothfulness. Yet no matter how hard Christians like that try, they never experience real peace about their Christian life. I remember a family friend who had been a Christian even before us. We attended the same church for many years. For whatever challenge in this person's Christian walk, they felt they were not being fulfilled. They left the church and started surfing around for churches. They would spend about six months in one church, then try another one for another nine months, then another until God ministered to them that there was nothing wrong with the churches they attended, but that they have allowed frustration of life to shift their belief in the truth of God's unchanging love for them.

Salvation, we all know, is a gift that we receive, not a reward to be earned. A person who tries even a little bit to gain salvation by works cannot become a Christian. Many Christians know that, and they preach it to unbelievers. The truth, therefore, is that the victory over any situation or challenge can't be based on our efforts; it comes only by the finished work of Jesus Christ. It is not a reward, but a gift. A person does not experience victory in the Christian life by trying hard to live for God, as it won't work. This is what Bible teacher Charles Trumbull describes as "spiritual frustration" in his book, *Victory in Christ.* Our friends, for example, are typical of many Christians. Instead of experiencing joy in Christ, they try to find fulfillment through their work and lifestyles. This led them to some spiritual frustration and fluctuations. Christianity is not about routine or service, but a relationship of Jesus Christ. If one is not careful, challenges of life, which the Lord Himself calls the "cares of this world", can derail anyone.

"Peace I leave with you, My peace I give you not as the world gives do I give to you. Let not your heart be troubled, neither let it be afraid." The Lord Jesus Christ says He has bequeathed to us. He has willed it to us as our inheritance. In Hebrew, "Shalom" is a very rich word which includes peace, as we know it in our English language. According to the Hebrew Lexicon (Brown Driver & Briggs) Shalom is described as completeness, safety, soundness of mind, welfare, health, prosperity, tranquility, contentment, peace in human relationships, peace with God in covenant relationship and peace from without and peace from war. This whole idea of peace is what Jesus meant when He said, "Peace I leave with you." It is the extravagant, prodigal love of the Father that can grant this kind of peace to us through Jesus Christ. Most of the time, believers have the tendency to pick and choose a little bit of the Shalom of God and forget about the whole and complete package as described in the definition.

Our forgiveness is hinged on the fact that God says He will have mercy on our unrighteousness. He will remember our sins no more because He has already put all of them on the body of His only begotten son, Jesus Christ. All of our sins have been forgiven not according to the sufficiency of our obedience or good work, but according to His riches in Christ Jesus (Colossians 2:13).

The key to enjoying success is not strenuous work, but spiritual rest. Many Christians feel like spiritual failures because they keep thinking like they are defeated; they keep working harder instead of resting more. Since I discovered this principle, I rest more in the promises of the Lord and no longer focus on my performance to measure my progress. I no longer measure my closeness to God by the number of chapters I read in the Bible every morning, or by the number of people I am able to witness to, however noble these Christian "duties" are. Initially, it is difficult not to, because the devil will keep reminding me that I have not done enough praying and fasting. Now, I allow His love to motivate me to do more reading of the scriptures and loving others more. I am reminded that a Christian is not one who dedicates his/her own work to God; rather, it is the story of God Himself doing the work through a person who is totally yielded to Him.

Trying to do something for God may sound admirable, but it produces damaging consequences. A grave example is the life of Abraham and Sarah, in the book of Genesis 15 and 16. After the promise of God to them of a child, they were excited; but as the years passed and Sarah didn't conceive, they decided to do the work of God for Him. Abraham went in with Hagar and brought forth Ishmael, not the promised son; but the descendants of the son of grace – Isaac that came later — and Ishmael (self-effort) are still at war today. Abraham and Sarah's efforts to help God only created problems for them and the world. Unfortunately, this war will never end until the Prince of Peace shows up again. Also, at the spiritual level, there is a war that rages in the hearts and lives of each of us daily. Do I rest on the promises of God, concerning the issues I am facing now, or do I rely on my work, smartness or integrity? This self-effort manifests in various forms. How can natural abilities become liabilities, you might ask? Whenever we rely on those abilities, instead of the One that gave us the abilities, this is another form of idol worshipping that might not be that obvious to us. Our daily prayer should be that God, Himself, will show us where we are depending on ourselves or resting on what Jesus has accomplished for us. Philippians 3:10: "That I may know Him and the power of His resurrection, and the fellowship of His sufferings, being conformed to His death." Learning to know Him and love Him is the cure for burnout.

As I was growing up, I remember my mom's saying, whenever she wanted to encourage me to do my best at school, "God helps those who help themselves." I am not discounting the importance of hard work or discipline; I am saying that but for the grace of God, we are insufficient on our own to help ourselves. This is still the philosophy of many Christians, with the conclusion that God will bless us as we "do our parts". Looking back on my life, the more I understand the grace walk, the more I recognize that all I have accomplished in life has only been possible by His grace. I never would have been satisfied with life if the focus of my Christian walk was on "doing work" to please God. I now experience peace, as I focus on the person of Jesus Christ. The little I am able to do is done with joy and gratitude to God, who has called me to be a co-laborer with Him.

I know now that Jesus Christ is interested in living His life through me, not in what I can do for Him: this is the difference between law and grace. Law says, "God, help me to keep your laws or rules; help me to do what you want me to do": whereas Grace will say, "Lord, express your life in me the way it pleases you." First Thessalonians 5:24: "He who calls you is faithful, who also will do it."

Because of His faithfulness, whatever He has called me to do will be done. He began the work of salvation in me and I am confident, therefore, that He will complete what He started.

We are saved to have intimacy with Him, as Adam and Eve had with Him at the beginning. He did not create us to "do" something for Him. Have you ever done something for somebody, only to find out that the person didn't like it anyway? Having grandchildren helps us to see deeper into the grace of God. Sometimes, my wife makes a certain kind of dish for our grandchildren, where she will put all her energy into making sure all of them would like and enjoy it. One of them in particular will just say, "I don't like it." Many believers will "do" a lot of work in an attempt to work for God to please their consciences, only to hear Him say, "I don't like it". Do good works have a place in the Christian life? Yes, of course, but it should be an overflow of our relationship with Him. It should be the fruit of righteousness, not from law or necessity. Being preoccupied with serving Christ, more than enjoying a relationship with Him, will lead to burnout, which many pastors and leaders go through very frequently. When one recognizes he or she is completely accepted by the beloved, there will be no stress in whatever one does. The more you have the revelation of Jesus love, the more you will be free to receive His complete forgiveness with no condemnation.

Luke 10:38-42:

> Now it happened as they went that He entered a certain village; and a certain woman named Martha welcomed Him into her house. And she had a sister called Mary, who also sat at Jesus' feet and heard His word. But Martha was distracted with much serving and she approached Him and said, "Lord, do you not care that my sister has left me to serve alone? Therefore, tell her to help me." And Jesus answered and said to her, "But Martha, Martha, you are worried and troubled about many things. But one thing is needed, and Mary has chosen that good part, which will not be taken away from her."

As a believer, do you recognize that ONE thing that is needed in your life? Are you constantly laboring for things that are of no value? All of us, one way or another, can testify to some things we have done in life that we can now say, "What a waste!" It could be a career we spent a lot of time and resources on that amounted to nothing. It could be a relationship we pursued for eternity that yielded nothing. In this story, Martha was very busy preparing food and service for the master, while Mary was resting. While Mary recognized the anointing around her, Martha was distracted away from Jesus by serving Him. Business in serving Christ can lead to lack of intimacy. Resting in Christ is the sole responsibility of Christians, as everything else flows out of that responsibility; that is the one thing needed.

If Jesus wanted a cup of water, as Mary was listening to Him, He would have asked instead of making spaghetti for Him with little or no attention to what He was saying. Maybe Jesus was not, at that point in time, interested in eating, but talking. Maybe at that time, Jesus was only interested in having a listening ear with a friend; or simply interested in fellowshipping not around any food, but in a heart-to-heart chat with a friend. Taking or receiving from Jesus pleases Him more than a life of service because in receiving from Him is when we know how to truly serve Him. In Matthew 20:28, Jesus says, "the Son of Man did not come to be served, but to serve, and to give His life a ransom for many."

Knowing who you are in Christ, or your identity in your Christian walk, is a prerequisite to your successful Christian life. If a person believes he is a tiger, nothing in the world can make him behave like a donkey. Many Christians have been deceived by others, either by their pastors, wives, or friends, into believing just what others want them to do. They follow the opinion of others about them rather than the leading of the inner man, their spirit.

Several times, I have been asked to be a pastor by friends and leaders in my former church. I don't know why they think I can be a pastor, when I don't have the witness in my spirit. It must be my look or the way I talk. Up till today, I have no clue why; because I did not have a witness of being a pastor in my spirit, I never consented to their opinions. Unfortunately, there are some people that have been "pushed" into a call that is not theirs; that you can observe that the call was not there because there are no fruits to show. (God is the judge. I don't say this in condemnation, only as an observation.) How, and why, do I say this? By their fruits we shall know them, the Bible says.

Many Christians have a spiritual inferiority complex. The perception of many Christians, especially those of us from Africa, is that we are not really serving God until we have many titles before and after our names. Among us, we must have prophet, prophetess, bishop, archbishop: down to lay reader and so on. What does this have to do with our identities in Christ? Knowing who we are and the purpose of our existence makes a great difference in our ability to rest on Christ. When you feel that you are not measuring up to what you perceive as your title, identity or call, there will be a tendency to believe that God does not like you, or you are no longer pleasing to Him. This is one of the reasons why some Christians find it difficult to rest in Christ, and instead they conjure many titles and prefixes to elongate their perceived callings. Rest in the Lord is a life of satisfaction in knowing we are complete in Him already. You are made righteous and clean by the blood of Jesus Christ, and it is His righteous standing that qualifies you. That is a life of rest that God wants His people to come to. Our identities as Christians are in our new, spiritual births, and not on what we do or our behavior. When we meet new friends, we introduce ourselves by what we do, our professions. At the end of our meeting, sometimes we exchange phone numbers and cards, most of the time with the purpose of contacting or connecting each other based on the identity we share. As Christians, our rest should be in our new spirits. 2 Corinthians 5:17: "Our identity is no longer found in the soul and body realm." If Jesus is at the core of our existence, that gives us an identity because we are in the family of God. I am fully accepted by God as I accept all my children with all their faults and differences. Their acceptance by me is not based on what they do to me or for me. In the same vein, my acceptance by God is not based on church activities, performances, or accomplishments. It is based only on believing His only begotten Son, Jesus Christ. His obedience and sacrifice is acceptable by the Father. Once I believe in Him, Jesus Christ,

God sees me as Him, and accepts me as He does Jesus.

Blessed be the likes of Billy Graham, Kenneth Hagin and many others of blessed memory that were never moved to obtain titles to prove anything to anyone, besides their simple faith in Him that called them to the ministry. (my personal observation).

Chapter 3

The Lavish Love of The Father In His Gift of Righteousness

Romans 5:17: "For if by the one man's offense death reigned through the one, much more those who receive abundance of grace and of the gift of righteousness will reign in life through the One, Jesus Christ."

The Word of God says that I became a sinner by the offense of one man (Adam), not by my own personal choice; thank God for providing a choice of a gift of righteousness through the last Adam – Jesus Christ. How can a sinner like me become righteous? It is the free gift of God to the world through His only begotten son, Jesus Christ.

It is free for anyone that received it by faith. I remember many years ago, my wife and I went to see the speaker of the House of Assembly of my state in Nigeria. It was towards the end of the year when many companies, corporations and various organizations, including politicians, give gifts to their friends, or any one in their "good" book. Because this assembly speaker was a relation of mine, we had the privilege to sit down with him in his personal office at the House of Assembly. Soon after we sat down, he called his personal secretary to take out some money in thousands to various clients and organizations as their gifts. While he sent fifty thousand to some, he sent only twenty-five thousand to others and even ten thousand to the rest. Before I could even ask him any questions about the disparity in his allocation of gifts, he said some of the media didn't write good things about them. So he gave the gifts according to the coverage, or non-coverage, the different news media gave him during the year.

Our prodigal Father does not give His gift of righteousness as humans do. He extravagantly gives this gift to men with no distinction of race, color, performance, work or circumstance, or obedience to law. He does not only provide this gift of righteousness; He gives the Holy Spirit to enable the believer in a way to please Him more than the law could ever have. It is God's righteousness at the expense of Christ. Jesus' righteousness has become my right to all the provisions and favor of God. 2 Corinthians 5:21 "For He made Him who knew no sin to become sin for us, that we might become the righteousness of God in Him."

We are not righteous by our actions. This statement usually sends some deep hmmms with many believers' minds. Right away, someone might ask, "So, if what I do does not matter, I can do what I want?" This kind of statement has robbed many people of the true understanding of God's love and His gift of righteousness. Our righteousness is based entirely on what Jesus did for us. His perfect sacrifice at Calvary made us righteous; any attempt to pay for it with our efforts and good deeds will only lead to frustrating the grace of God, as the apostle Paul says in Galatians 2:21: "I do not frustrate the grace of God, for if righteousness came by the law (works) then Christ is dead in vain."

It is not based on our right-doing. Our doing right may come up later, because we love God first because He first loved us. Our love to Him does not come first; our doing work or doing good deeds does not come first; our motivation to do any good work should be the fruit of His righteousness in us. We say "Thank you" after someone has given us a gift, not before.

God's righteousness is free for all, but it cost Jesus Christ the pains and sufferings He went through on the way to Calvary and His death on the cross. God paid for it with the blood of His only begotten Son, Jesus Christ.

The extravagance or prodigal love of the Father is manifested in this that His son, who knew no sin, will become my sin bearer on the cross. He did this so that humanity, which is born of sin and filled with sins, can now become the righteousness of God.

Understanding of this love of God leads to boldness in coming to God, as the Holy Scriptures encourage believers to do in Hebrews 4:13: "Let us therefore come boldly to the throne of grace that we may obtain mercy and find grace to help in time of need."

According to Apostle Frederick K. C. Price in his book, *How to Obtain Strong Faith*, "Knowing the reality of our righteousness in Christ" is one sure way of obtaining a strong faith. There is no degree of righteousness; once you receive this gift, it is once and for all. God sees me righteous when I am low or high in my faith walk with Him. He sees me righteous when I feel like it or when I don't feel like it. My righteousness is not by my feelings. It is a gift from God based solely on what Jesus Christ has accomplished. All that is required of me therefore is to believe and receive it by faith.

According to Paul the apostle in Philippians 3:8-9:

> ...Yet indeed I also count all things loss for the excellent of the knowledge of Christ Jesus my Lord for whom I have suffered the loss of all thing, and count them rubbish, that I may gain Christ and be found in Him, not having my own righteousness which is from the law, but that which is through faith in Christ, the righteousness which is from God by faith.

The righteousness by law is when you base your relationship with God on what you do for Him or your obedience to His law, especially with the Ten Commandments. When you think you have obeyed the law based on your own human judgment, you have more confidence in God and then expect your prayers to be answered. At other times, when you fail to obey the law to the letter, your confidence to receive any answer to your prayers from God is shaken. His righteousness alone is what guarantees God's grace and favor. You don't need to do anything for God to accept you; your acceptance is based on what Jesus did. You can't undo it or improve on it to be more acceptable by God. In Ephesians 1:6, Apostle Paul writes, "...to the praise of the glory of His grace, by which He made us accepted in the Beloved. In Him we have redemption through His blood, the forgiveness of sins, according to the riches of His grace."

In 1 Corinthians 1:2, Paul calls the believers there holy and saints. Was Paul referring to the same groups in later chapters, like Chapters 5 and 11? The groups' behavior in those chapters does not sound holy or saintly. For example, 1 Corinthians 5:1 says, "It is actually reported that there is sexual immorality among you, and such sexual immorality as is not even named among the Gentiles-that a man has his father's wife!" Also in Chapter 11, Paul also was amazed at the division, factions and politics of recognition in the church of Corinth. Paul, however, called them saints because he was referring to what God calls them and how God sees them, because of the imputation of the righteousness of Jesus Christ. In later chapters, he admonished them to live and behave like their calls. He wanted them to remember that the nature of Christ in them should be lived out. Ephesians 4:24 says, "and that you put on the new man which was created according to God, in true righteousness and holiness." When you know what you have, and use it appropriately, you will get the desired result. Paul says that because the Ephesians had been given the new spirit in true righteousness and holiness, they could live a godly life that was pleasing to God: "Awake to righteousness, and sin not." Awake to your true nature, the God nature and spirit in you.

The Lord Jesus Christ is our righteousness, as 2 Corinthians 5:21 states: "For He made Him who knew no sin to be sin for us, that we might become the righteousness of God in Him." What you are at your spirit level determines your real identity. Many preachers chase after shadows by emphasizing living right in most of their sermons, without teaching on the understanding of Christian identity. As a saint in the family of God, once I know that God loves me so much and gave His best for me, I will desire to live right; in accordance to who I am. I am the righteousness of God in Christ Jesus: I am a saint; I am God's workmanship; I am holy, and I am fully accepted by God. Knowing this should make one feel like shouting! How about you, child of God? Each moment I remember who I am in Christ Jesus, I want to walk according to that call; I want to walk worthy of my identity; I want to walk according to the purpose in my life.

The Church at large has always taught sin-consciousness rather than righteous-consciousness. We have been taught that we are weak, sinful, and unworthy until most prayers have become: "Before we ask anything from the Father, let us confess our sins", followed by "God, oh God, have mercy upon our poor souls." There is nothing wrong with a cry for mercy, but it must not be born out of a heart of fear. Calling to an embrace of sin-consciousness every time we want to fellowship with the Father, in prayer, creates an evil conscience. When a person becomes born again, a child of God, he has the nature of God. This means God's life is in him, and this gives him a right relationship with God. Reminding God of what He has already promised to forget each time we come to Him in prayer is not a sign of humility, but ignorance of the Word and promises of a faithful Father. When my father was alive, I can't remember anytime I went to him for any request by starting to confess my sins of omission or commission; and he never denied me of my request, unless he did not have it. Could our Heavenly Father do more than our earthly fathers? I don't only think so; I know so. Hebrews 4:16 says, "Let us therefore come boldly to the throne of grace, that we may obtain mercy and grace to help in the time of need." Coming to confession at every prayer meeting is not a way to come boldly. God does not want us to come with timidity, but boldly because our righteousness is not based on our performances. It is based on what Jesus has done.

Romans 8:1-2 says, "There is therefore now no condemnation to those who are in Christ Jesus, who do not walk according to the flesh, but according to the Spirit. For the law of the Spirit of life in Christ Jesus has made me free from the law of sin and death." Even when no one lays a charge against someone, some people lay charges on themselves day after day by reminding God that they are unworthy to come to Him. Even when God has made it clear that they have been justified and declared righteous by the sacrifice of His only begotten Son, they make God out to be a liar. They make Him a liar by constantly reminding Him to remember their sins. Some preachers have taught that confession of our sins was a proof of our goodness.

Is there a place for confession of sins; yes, of course. 1 John 1:8-9 writes about this, giving us the assurance that the blood of Jesus Christ cleanses us from all sin. I am saying that I don't read it anywhere in the New Covenant that each time we go the Father in prayer, we should remind God that we are sinners and unworthy children. Rather, the Word of God wants us to come boldly to the throne of grace to obtain mercy and find grace to help in time of need. If God has not made provision, whereby we can live without condemnation, then He has not truly delivered us; but thank God for His complete package of salvation. We have a new relationship with the Father: we are His children; we have a new Father; the devil is no longer our master. We stand before our Father God complete. We are filled with His fullness (John 1: 16).

Righteousness creates the ability to stand in the presence of a holy God fearlessly, as though sin and failure have never occurred in our lives; that is the message of grace from the Prodigal Father.

A proper understanding of our identity in Christ is sufficient motivation to have a completely different attitude toward sin. This understanding does not lead me to a sinful life, but rather it empowers me to live a holy life. The Bible says that I am a new creation in Christ Jesus, and I believe it by faith. Because I believe this, I don't have to act or perform to prove it to anybody. Some Christians struggle with sins, because they have believed its lie.

Satan, the great deceiver, has caused them to believe that they are really not new creators, and they believe this lie of the enemy. Not until they believe in the identities of a Christian I have enumerated above will they be able to go on the offensive against Satan and overcome sin. I am not in any way trying to convey the idea that my understanding of my identity in Christ has caused me to live a sinless life. I do know now, however, that if I sin, I quickly see the foolishness of my act because I will sense the contradiction of such an action against my new identity. I will quickly, with the same breath, call on the Father about my sin and ask for His forgiveness. The Holy Spirit within me will convict me of my identity or position, that is, my righteousness in Christ. This will cause me to look into the Greater One in me to overcome the sin.

The life of Lot, the nephew of Abraham, is another example of the way God sees the people He has called into His family of faith. What can we say about the life of Lot? The Bible records that Lot was a drunk, and he impregnated his two daughters. In 2 Peter 2:7-8, God calls him righteous! God must have forgotten about his past, or God has something in mind. How can Lot be considered righteous? Are we talking about the same man? In the Old Testament, God responded to the faith of those that believed Him by imputing righteousness to them in spite of their not perfect characters. (Rom. 4:3). The same God that imputed righteousness to Abraham did so to Lot, despite his contradictory actions. Maybe the difference in the lives of Abraham and Lot was the former understood his identity in God and walked in it, while the latter did not really walk in it. Instead, he believed, like other nations around him, that he, too, was an ordinary person like them.

The totality of our lives as Christians is in Jesus Christ: not about Him, not about various activities for Him, but Christ Himself. 2 Peter 1:3-4 says:

> As His divine power has given to us all things that pertain to life and godliness, through the knowledge of Him who called us by glory and virtue, by which have been given to us exceedingly great and precious promises, that through these you may be partakers of the divine nature, having escaped the corruption that is in the world through lust.

At the deeper level of our identities as Christians is Christ; He has become our life. Because He lives in us, He desires to express His life through us. Allowing Jesus to live His life through us makes the yoke easy, for doing it on our own will always lead to frustration, failure and un-fulfillment.

Chapter 4

The Lavish Love of the Father in the Gift of the Holy Spirit

From one step to another, God abundantly provides every need for His creation, so that His goodness can bring us back to Him. He provides extravagantly for all our daily sustenance, the basic necessities of life: our planet is conducive for human habilitation; there is plenty of water to quench our thirsts; there is plenty of food to fill our stomachs. I am talking on general terms here. I am not unaware of some uncommon situations around the world where there is famine, war and many other circumstances that make it hard for some people to access these God-given provisions. In the same manner, once a sinner receives the Lord Jesus Christ as his/her personal savior, that is he is born again, the Lord makes a provision of another helper, a comforter for him or her. Even though you don't have to be filled with the Holy Spirit to be saved or born again, there is a free gift, in the form of a helper, that the Father has provided to all that have believed Him. Unfortunately, there are many believers who have received the Holy Spirit, but don't know the importance of Him because they doubt, or they are ignorant, of the Holy Spirit's power.

1 John 4:4 reads, "You are of God, little children, and have overcome them, because He who is in you is greater than he who is in the world." The Holy Spirit in a believer's heart is greater than Satan in the world.

This has nothing to do with how we feel. It is believing and receiving that has given me the empowering spirit of God in me, which will not allow me to fail because He is greater than any other power in the world. God lives and manifests His power through people, especially believers that are confident of who is in them.

One must be endowed by the power of the Holy Spirit to be an effective witness for Jesus.

At new birth, Jesus Christ, by His spirit, takes residence in us. We are baptized into the Body of Christ by His Spirit; after that, Jesus baptizes us with the Holy Spirit.

At this stage, the well that was established at conversion burst open to become rivers of living waters. Like a dam gushes out to turn the turbans and generate electricity (power), so is the dam or pool of His Spirit in us at the new birth bursting out to become the river of living waters that produce the power needed for a fruitful, peaceful and holy life.

Have you heard about being burned out before, in reference to the service in the kingdom? I am not talking about physical exhaustion, but I am talking of the spiritual aspect of our service. The main reason why Christians become worn out is the reliance on self-effort, but if one depends on the Holy Spirit within, the energizer, the power sources, the flowing river, spiritual weakness will be a thing of the past. The Lord does not want us to serve Him in our strength. Our Prodigal Father has provided the power necessary for lifelong service. My pastor, Apostle Price, is still going strong at eighty-three years and can still minister the Word nonstop for hours in any conference. I don't want to be misunderstood here; that any other pastor is not able to do what I am writing about should not be seen as a put-down. I am only encouraging believers that our Father has extravagantly supplied all that we need to serve in holiness and godliness before Him all the days of our lives.

The Holy Spirit is given freely by grace to help and enable us to move on into the deeper areas of our Christian experience, and to achieve victory in our daily lives for Christ. This gift of the Holy Spirit is not given as an attainment or reward based on any degree of holiness, but on the love of the Father to all that believe in His Son, Jesus Christ. Thanks be to

God for His inexpressible gift. As a new believer in the early 80s, we were taught that before we received the Holy Spirit, we must first have lived a holy life. Nothing can be farther from the truth, because it is with the help of the Holy Spirit we can put our lives together.

Like the gift of righteousness, the gift of the indwelling of the Holy Spirit is an unmerited gift – it is the grace or favor of God to His children. Before Jesus Christ left this earth to go back to heaven, He told His disciples, in John 14:16-18: **whom the world cannot receive, because it neither sees Him nor knows Him:**

"I will pray the Father and He will give you another Helper, that He may abide with you forever-the Spirit of truth: but you know Him, for He dwells with you. I will not leave you orphans; I will come to you." It is unfortunate that some Christians still argue that to be born-again is the same thing as receiving the Holy Spirit. If that is true, then in the quoted passages, Jesus Christ says, "Whom the world cannot receive, because it neither sees Him nor knows Him". Before anybody became a Christian, he or she was in the world without the ability to see or know Jesus in a spiritual sense. How can such a person then receive the Holy Spirit? To receive the Holy Spirit, you must first be born again; that is the way the heavenly Father has set up His plan.

Jesus' promise to His disciples is that He would not leave them comfortless or as orphans. His extravagant love provides for our future, because He knows that to live in this world of sin and pain, we need help. We need guidance; we need a teacher; we need a comforter when we are down.

1 John 4:4 reads, "You are of God, little children, and have overcome them, because He who is in you is greater than he that is in the world." The Holy Spirit is the greater one in anyone that has freely received the gift of the Holy Spirit and, of course, the Spirit of Christ while Satan is that one in the world. Because

of the greater one in me, I am an overcomer; I will not be defeated. I believe that, and act like it is so. I do not walk by sight, but in faith of what the Word says. Many Christians are moved by what is happening around them. If somebody dies suddenly of whatever circumstance, they start to panic and fear that they are prone to such an end, too. Most of the time Christians forget about the gift of the greater one in them. If for whatever reason death comes, they throw themselves down in sorrow like the people of the world, forgetting the admonition in the Bible that says, "I do not want you to be ignorant, brethren concerning those who have fallen asleep, lest you sorrow as others who have no hope" (1 Thess. 4:13). His spirit lives in the heart of every believer, for the Word says, "I will never leave you nor forsake you" (Heb. 13:5). Not until you have the realization of His Spirit in you, and begin to rely on Him, you will not be an effective witness for Him in your daily walk with Him. "I can do all things through Christ, which strengthened me," (Phil. 4:13). His strength is by the way of the Holy Spirit.

Being saved or born again is not the same as being baptized in the Holy Spirit. As I indicated earlier, Jesus baptizes us in the Holy Spirit. As Jesus baptizes us into the Body as a gift of salvation, then we receive the gift of the Holy Spirit, the gift for power. When the well of water starts to spring up with an everlasting flow of life, no one will be able to curtail it or stop it. Jesus used His encounter with the Samaritan woman at the well to illustrate this point. He wanted to lead His own into a deeper understanding of salvation and the indwelling spirit that will empower believers. The Bible records this encounter as something that Jesus needed to do; John 4:4, "But He needed to go through Samaria." Even though this was a longer route from Judea to Galilee, He needed to go through it anyway for the sake of this important lesson that He wanted to teach believers. Even though the Jews didn't have any fellowship or interactions with the Samaritans, Jesus still decided to pass through Samaria because of the prodigal love of the Father for His children; John 4:5:

> So, He came to a city of Samaria called Sychar where Jacob well was. It was at this well that a woman of Samaria came to draw water at noon time. Jesus said to her, "Give me a drink," but the woman responded, "How is it that you being a Jew ask a drink from me a Samaritan woman?" Jesus answered and said to her, "If you knew the gift of God and who it is who says to you 'Give me a drink,' you would have asked Him and he would have given you living water." Jesus answered and said to her, "Whoever drinks of this water will thirst again, but whoever drinks of the water that I shall give him will never thirst. But the water

that I shall give him will become in him a fountain of water springing up into everlasting life."

The continuous flow of the spirit of God in us gives the empowerment to bear fruits. Towards the end of the woman's conversation with Jesus Christ, He made it clear to her in verse 24, "God is Spirit, and those who worship Him must worship in spirit and truth." No one can worship God in spirit without the presence of the Holy Spirit in him/her. People do worship in so many ways and forms, but the acceptable worship of God is through the spirit. Our prayers, for example, are limited to our understanding of a particular issue. However, we have an advocate that intercedes on our behalf, with groaning that cannot be uttered (Rom. 8:26). The gift of praying in tongues is one of the underused gifts that the Prodigal Father has given to His children. I have encountered so many situations in life where I don't even have a clue of what exactly I should ask the Father, or even how to do the asking. I know I can pray in the name of Jesus Christ, but how do I tap into my innermost being? This is the challenge. Even sometimes when I know exactly what I am asking, I still feel inadequate in my language choice of words or even sometimes with daydreams on unrelated issues. Am I the only mortal person among believers? Please forgive me if I expose some of you also.

In such a confused state of our minds like this, the Lord wants us to pull out the spiritual gift of praying in the spirit to get the job done. He helps our weaknesses, and He who knows and searches our hearts, knowing the mind of the Spirit. He makes intercession for the saints, according to the will of God. Allow the Holy Spirit to pray through you. If you are at a loss of what to do, or too weary to pray about any situation, the Word of God says that the Holy Spirit will make intercession for you in your weakness. You can tell Him that you don't know what to do about the situation. You can tell Him that you are weak; He knows already. You can ask Him to help you pray the perfect and acceptable prayer to the Father but come boldly to Him with the expectation and trust that He will do what the Father has promised in His Word. When you do that, and start to pray in tongues with the "groaning that cannot be uttered", you are actually releasing the Holy Spirit to pray through you. When the Holy Spirit prays in and through you, you can be confident that you are praying a powerful prayer. I am of the opinion that screaming, shouting and doing some silly stuff is not a powerful prayer that touches the heart of God.

Praying in tongues allows you to release the power of the Holy Spirit in every circumstance. When you and I pray in our known language, either English, Spanish, or any local language, our prayers are limited by what we know. Even though believers usually quote, "...we walk by faith, not by sight", most of our prayers are based on our feelings.

When we pray in tongues, we eliminate the desires of the flesh, which is mostly based on sight because the Holy Spirit is not limited in any way to what we see or feel. He, alone, is the one that can pray effectively to release the desired miracle or result. The Holy Spirit who sees and knows all things and understands perfectly what the root of the problem is, will pray the perfect will of the Father.

Praying in tongues leads you, as a believer, into a place of spiritual rest and refreshment.

Isaiah 28:9-12:

> Whom will he teach knowledge? And whom will he make to understand the message? Those just weaned from milk? Those just drawn from breast? For precept must be upon precept, precept upon precept, Line upon line, line upon

line, Here a little, there a little. For with stammering lips and another tongue He will speak to this people, To whom He said, "This is the rest with which you may cause the weary to rest" And this is the refreshing, Yet they would not hear.

Again, the Lord echoes the same thing in chapter 30:15, "For thus says the Lord God, the Holy One of Israel: In returning and rest you shall be saved: In quietness and confidence shall be your strength."

The problem with many believers is that because they do not understand what they are saying or praying, they don't believe that they are talking to God; and as such, they don't expect any answers or results of their prayers.

Jesus told His disciples, in Acts 1:8, "But you shall receive power when the Holy Spirit has come upon you; and you shall be witnesses to Me in Jerusalem, and in all Judea and Samaria, and to the end of the earth." Toward the end of the Samaritan woman's encounter with Jesus, nothing can be more dramatic of a life being touched by Jesus Christ and demonstration of the enabling power of the Holy Spirit. I understand that the Holy Spirit has not been given at this stage. as Jesus said in John 7:37-39; this was a future event that was relevant at her time. For example, she received the power to be a witness right there and then. This was a woman that came to the well at noon time, who did not want the gossipers of her days to see her during the early morning or evening at the well when most women went to the well. She, instead, went alone at midday; "it was about the sixth hour." After her time with Jesus Christ, she not only left her water pot and went back to the city, but was bold enough to invite the men to "come and see a man who told her all things that I ever did". The Bible records that many of the Samaritans of that city believed in Him, because of the word of the woman. She had been empowered to be a witness for the Lord.

The Lavish Love of the Father Provides a Helper, the Holy Spirit.
John 14:16-26

Because of the extravagant love of the Father for His children, Jesus promised His disciples that He would pray to the Father to give them another helper that will abide with them _forever._ Unfortunately, some believers think that the Holy Spirit comes and goes, depending on how holy they are at a particular time. I choose to believe the words of Jesus, rather than the opinions of man. Jesus Christ says that the Holy Spirit will abide with us forever. He did not say only when we are doing good or are holy. He says forever, even when I feel holy or dirty. His abiding with me does not depend on how holy I feel at a particular time. Actually, I should recognize His presence more when I am down, so that I can call for His assistance and help.

Recently I noticed a gift, a present, I was given by a friend during one celebration over ten years ago that I never opened. You can attest to it that sometimes we forget to open a gift for a long time. If it is a perishable gift, we then throw it away. Sometimes the gift might have outlived its usefulness, or we outgrow it in size. The gift of the Holy Spirit is never perishable, outlived or irrelevant. Regrettably, some believers will get to heaven before they know the value of the Holy Spirit in their lives. In the book of Isaiah, there was a prophesy of the new world that said, "And the Lord will wipe away tears from all faces." Could this be in relation to some of the gifts the Father gave to us extravagantly, but that we were ignorant of or refuse to receive? At that time, it would be too late to use the gifts because there will be no need for them anymore, for we will see Him as He is. God gave us His Holy Spirit to teach us all things and to bring to our remembrance all things that Jesus has taught us. The Holy Spirit is a gift from our Father God to help us in our Christian walk.

John 16:13: "The Holy Spirit, the spirit of truth, will guide you into all truth." People all over the world are seeking the truth. It is unfortunate that people run to places where there is no truth. Some run to ordinary human wisdom, and they call it truth. Every religion has what it considers its own way or truth.

1 John 2:20, 27:

> But you have an anointing from the Holy One, and you know all things. V.27 But the anointing which you have received from Him abides in you, and you do not need that anyone teach you; but as the same anointing teaches you concerning all things, and is true, and is not a lie, and just as it has taught you, you will abide in Him.

As a child of God, His continuous teaching through the Holy Spirit is provided when you follow directions of the Holy Spirit within. You won't have a troubled mind; rather, you will witness His peace.

Chapter 5

The Lavish Love of the Father in Abundant Supply of Every Resource

Good knowledge and opinion of God brings increased faith into one's life. When you meditate or bring into remembrance all of God's benefits, faith will rise up to face any other challenge. This is what David referred to in Psalm 119:99: "I have more understanding than all my teachers, For Your testimonies are my meditation." He says further in Psalm 103:1-5:

> Bless the Lord, O my soul, and all that is within me, bless His holy name! Bless the Lord O my soul and forget not all His benefits: Who forgives all your iniquities, who heals all your diseases, who redeems your life from destruction, who

crowns you with loving-kindness and tender mercies, who satisfies your mouth with good things, so that your youth is renewed like the eagle's.

It is almost inconceivable to think that since we accept Jesus as our Savior, we are joint heirs with Him! A joint heir shares equally in an inheritance; this means I do not lack anything that Jesus has. Our adoption as children makes us joint heirs together with Him; it is this adoption that makes it possible for us to put on the righteousness of God. This righteousness is not second or third class, but is the same righteousness that Jesus has because God has made us joint heirs together with Him. Even when the psalmist was not aware of what the Lord had in stock for His children through Jesus Christ, he said through the spirit, in Psalm 68:19, "Bless the Lord, who daily loads us with benefits, the God of our salvation." How precious also are the thoughts of this God to us!

We are no longer servants of God, but children (Gal. 4:7). Our service to Him now is in appreciation of what He has done for us in Jesus Christ.

If the saints of old, like Moses and Elijah, were servants of God, we can only imagine the power that lies within us as children of God! Many believers have the opinion that Jesus is the only Son of God; yes, the only begotten, but we are His adopted children with the same inheritance as Jesus. In Romans 8:25, Jesus is referred to as the firstborn of many brethren. If you are born again, you are one of many brethren.

Galatians 4:4-7 says:

> But when the fullness of the time had come, God sent forth His Son, born of a woman, born under the law, to redeem those who were under the law, that we

might receive the adoption as sons. And because you are sons, God has sent forth the Spirit of His Son into your hearts, crying out, "Abba, Father!" Therefore, you are no longer a slave but a son, and if a son, then an heir of God through Christ.

It is not robbery to say that we are joint heirs with Jesus Christ. God wants us to have that consciousness and walk in it; it is the prodigal love of the Father for us.

Philippians 2:5-6 says the same of Jesus Christ. We are not depriving God of His glory, nor taking anything away from Jesus for saying that we are joint heirs with Him. That is the truth that God wants us to have, so that we can be made free. The more we think like Jesus, the more we can accomplish for His glory on this earth.

John 1:3

"All things were made through Him and without Him nothing was made that was made." He made all things and gave man dominion over them (Gen. 1:26)

God wants us to invest our abilities to create value on all the things He has provided freely for us on earth. He wants us to plant, sow and build. He wants us to heal, invest and invent things that bless people and cause His kingdom on earth to flourish (Col 3:17).

Psalm 68:19 says, "Blessed be the Lord who daily loads us with benefits, the God of our salvation!" Our prodigal father loads us with benefits of His love daily. Because of the myopic way man looks at things around him, there is always a tendency to overlook the abundance of God's blessings everywhere we turn. Let us look into some of these free gifts our Father has provided for our use.

Natural resources are all that exists without the actions of human beings. These are naturally occurring substances or materials that can be used for economic purposes.

According to *The New Book of Knowledge Encyclopedia,* The mineral resources of the Pacific Ocean alone, for example, are enormous and inexhaustible. Salt, bromine and magnesium have been mined from there. Vast deposits of natural gas also exist there.

The ocean is one of Earth's most valuable natural resources, provided freely by God. Iron, copper, nickel, cobalt and many others can be found in the deep sea. Crude oil lay in billions of metric tons under the ocean, most of which has not be touched.

Marine life in the Ocean like salmon, cod, lobster, crab, shrimp and seaweed are processed for food. Some other natural resources of the ocean are:

- Medicine from animals or oceans planks
- Seafood (we eat)

- Household items (salt, toothpaste has kelp)
- Oceans absorptions (carbon dioxide, reducing the carbon dioxide left in the air we breathe)
- Oceans moderate temperatures, cools hot areas during the day and releases that heat at night.

Over seventy percent of the earth is covered by water, which are mostly oceans. Importance of water as a natural resource cannot be over-emphasized. Human beings and animals can't survive without water.

Drinking, cleaning, washing of clothes, utensils, watering plants and irrigations are some of the essential uses of water.

There are more than 376 million trillion gallons of water on earth.

In our modern days, the most significant use of water, besides drinking, is to produce hydropower by harnessing its energy.

The ocean environment holds a wealth of resources that we rely on, from fuel sources to food supplies. Most of our oil and gas reserves lie beneath the sea floor, and many are yet to be discovered. Around the world, more people are relying on food from the seas and oceans.

Oceans are sources for a number of useful resources, and as the resources available are being unutilized, the demand for various resources is increasing, due to the ever-increasing population. In future, it is the ocean that human beings will turn to for more supply of various types of resources.

Oceans are an importance source of a number of food items. It is believed that they can meet the food requirements of mankind for a long time.

Fish, the most important component of the food resources of the oceans, also constitutes a major economic activity:

Medicines from the ocean

Ocean exploration often leads to new ideas, including new medicines. Researchers are exploring the oceans depths for new medications to treat cancer, viruses, heart diseases, etc. The seas contain an uncounted number of species of plants and animals. These creatures provide a vast storehouse of chemical compounds that are unknown on land. Chemicals and biological materials now are in use or being developed, including anti-cancer drugs, drugs to fight inflammation, tuberculosis, HIV and malaria.

Mineral Resources

The Earth's crust contains useful mineral resources. Scientists have identified more than 3000 different minerals in the Earth's crust. Only a few of them have been mined for human use. Gold, silver, and aluminum copper are common metals that exist as nuggets of pure metal. They are prized for their beauty and rarity. Subsurface, surface, undersea mining provide millions of jobs all over the world with uncountable "free" money.

Fossil Fuels

Natural resources like coal, petroleum and natural gas are formed from the remains of living things millions of years ago.

Globally, fossil fuels, like minerals, are one of the main sources of energy. Crude oil or unrefined petroleum is used in the production of synthetic fabrics, medicines waxes, synthetic rubber, insecticides, chemical fertilization, detergents, shampoos, and many other products.

Coal, the most abundant fossil fuel in the world, is found on every continent. Coal for many centuries was the main source of energy in many parts of the world. When scientists discovered that atoms had smaller fundamental parts, they wondered if atoms could be split into even smaller parts. Many years later, after a series of research and tests, scientists were able to split the nuclei of heavy atoms. This splitting of the nucleus of a large atom into smaller nuclei is called nuclear fission. The forces that hold the nucleus of an atom together are more than one million times stronger than the strongest chemical bonds between atoms. Even today, scientists are still in awe of what holds the nucleus together. All things that scientists have not been able to find answers to are right there in the Word of God. For example, for thousands of years, no one knew that the earth was spherical; explorers had always believed that the earth was flat. Had they asked God, He would have referred them to Job 38:6,16 and Isaiah 40:22 for the answer. In Colossians 1:16-18, God provides the answer; it says: "For by Him all things were created that are in heaven and on earth, visible and invisible, whether thrones or dominions or principalities or powers. All things were created through Him and for Him. And He is before all things, and in Him, all things consist." Jesus

Christ is the one that holds everything together because He created them all.

Solar Energy

Many scientists believe that the human race must eventually rely on the sun for most of its energy needs if they want to survive. Recently, there has been a lot of uncertainty with the price of oil in the world market. For some periods, the price might be too high, while in another period, too low. Each period creates its own unique problems, but God, by His generous provision, has remained consistent in His abundant supply of all that we need as humans. Every fifteen minutes, for example, the Earth receives enough energy from the sun to meet the energy needs of the whole world for one year! According to the U.S Department of Energy, the energy that reaches us from the sun is about 160 times more than we use from all other sources.

This is so incredible when one considers the fact that the earth receives only a fraction of the sunrays because of the distance. Most of our energy sources are fossil fuels or fuels that come from the remains of living things that lived long ago. Once we finished such fuels, they will be gone forever. The sun, however, is expected to burn for another five billion years. It could be pointed out here that the sun is just one of many trillion stars in the universe but happens to be the closest. For centuries, people have known that the sun's energy can be harnessed. Over 2000 years ago, the Greeks made huge, mirror-like panels and used them to bounce the sunrays off to burn down enemy ships according to Encyclopedia Americana, International Edition.

Today, scientists around the world are devising many better uses for solar energy. Homes, office buildings, factories, and entire communities are being powered by pollution-free solar energy.

How great is our prodigal Father with such inexhaustible riches? He provides not only spiritual gifts but also materials blessings.

Chapter 6

The Lavish Love of the Father in Eternal Life, The Home Going

When people start to advance in age, I have observed that they tend to talk more about old friends, with reference to their places of origin. I have heard some African American families, who grew up in the South, constantly talk about going back home after they have lived for over forty years in other parts of the country. Some would say that they would like to go back to the South to retire. Do they think that the South is economically or socially better than where they are now? Not necessarily, but they feel a pull towards "home".

This longing desire is not only peculiar to this group of people. Recently, I can't remember how I got sucked into a group of some old friends that I went to high school within the late

60s and early 70s in Nigeria. Now, they desired that we form alumni associations with the main objective of meeting to talk and fellowship about our years together as teenagers. During those years, we never thought there would be any reason for us to think together or even desire to be close again. Now, this has become our priority, even to the point of spending thousands of dollars yearly to achieve this goal.

As aging is becoming more and more pronounced, people naturally gravitate toward their old pals and the people they grew up with. Is this an indication of the way God has fashioned His creation? Is there a home to go back to for the final celebration?

I have been in America for about four decades now. By the grace of God, I have been relatively comfortable here. Many of the amenities that are not readily available in Nigeria, my country, like constant flow of electricity, good roads, pipe-bored water, safety, and many other things, are available in

America. Yet, there is a longing in my heart to be in Nigeria. Home exercises a powerful influence over every human being. Even though I have been able to go to Nigeria at least once a year over the past twenty years, each time I spend a lot of money on airfare, gifts, and other expenses. The desire to be there is unquenchable. The memories of times, friends, places, and events that happened when I was growing up there will just not leave me. Each time I get there, even though the memories of the past are nourishing to me, I am always disappointed at the way things are. Despite my disappointments, there remains a deep longing within me to be back again and again.

The human race is a band of exiles trying to go home. Right from Adam's sin of wanting to be like God, to Jacob cheating on his brother and running away to exile for years. Jacob craved to be back home with his brother. Jacob's son, Joseph, was in the land of Egypt where they were enslaved for four hundred and thirty years, still wanted to go back home. When the whole nation was exiled again to Babylon, the yearnings were there to go back home. Even when they returned, but were controlled by Greece, Syria, and other nations, the desire to return to the Promised Land (Palestine) never left them. The Jews never felt satisfied or at home in any other place besides the Promised Land. The prophets made up their minds that God made clear to them. For example, Isaiah is a miniature version of the Bible, with sixty-six chapters corresponding to the sixty-six books of the Bible. The first thirty-nine books deal with law and judgment, while twenty-seven chapters in the second section deal with messages of mercy, salvation, comfort, and eternal restoration through the Messiah, the Lord Jesus Christ. The message of the Bible is that the human race is a band of exiles trying to return home.

The prophecies of Jeremiah and Hosea warn backsliders of the dangers of forgetting that the day is coming for the great gathering of God's people. Even with the judgment of Babylonian captivity for seventy years, worldwide dispersion, there will be a final re-gathering of God's people.

Ezekiel was commissioned to rebuke Israel in captivity for her many sins. He warned them of further judgment of God, revealing a future restoration of the nation and the eternal reign of their Messiah on earth because the Lord will be there.

Even though Amos explained the consequences of sin, he did not forget to encourage the people that there will be a re-gathering and restoration of God's people.

Jonah is the story of a bigoted Jew who, after being chastened by the Lord for disobedience, preached to and converted the whole city of Nineveh. This book shows why the destruction of Nineveh and the Assyrian empire was delayed; this further illustrates God's mercy and goodness. He does not want ANY sinner to perish, but to come to repentance and acknowledge Jesus as his/her Lord and Savior. Many sermons we hear today seem to contradict this; it is like God really enjoys the death and destruction of sinners, but my Bible says that it is the goodness of God that brings man to repentance. That goodness of God is all that this book has tried to point out in various ways. God is not slack concerning His promises, but He delays His coming so that more people will be ready to come to the great feast He is preparing for His people.

To warn all men and invite all men to this last feast, this merciful God uses everything He created to woo or draw all men back to Himself. When that seems insufficient, He caused His only begotten Son to be the ransom for the sin of the world. Jonah knew how merciful this God could be; that was why he fled from His sight. He did not want God to warn the people of Ninevah, which would show mercy.

All these prophets express the ultimate purpose of God in all His dealings to bring Israel and mankind back to the place of conformity to His eternal will and plan so that the blessings He originally promised man may be finally and completely fulfilled.

This world, as it now exists, is not the home we long for; a real, final home is awaiting us. All the mini-exoduses and mini-homecomings of the Bible have proved not to be the real thing. Jesus came to bring the human race home.

By the time Jesus died, He was crucified outside the gates of the city as a powerful symbol of rejection by His own people. He even cried at the time of death, "My God, my God, why have you forsaken me?" (Matt. 27:46), which was a tremendous cry of spiritual rejection and homelessness. Jesus will make the world a perfect home for us again, like the Garden of Eden was perfect without sin. The Father God will come and meet us, embrace us and bring us to the feast. We will be no strangers there because it will be a familiar sight.

He came to experience the exile and rejection that we deserve. He came to experience the full curse of human rebellion and homelessness so that we could be welcomed into our true home.

Our God will return one day to take us home (Isaiah 35:9-10). In the end, there is going to be a feast, the marriage supper of the Lamb (Rev. 19:9). The New Jerusalem, the city of God, will come down out of heaven to fill the earth (Rev. 21:10). Then the whole earth will become the Garden of Eden, where death, decay, suffering, and the yearning for another home will be gone. The Lord, Himself, will wipe away all tears from our eyes, and there will be no more death or mourning or crying or pain. For the old order of things has passed away (Rev. 21:4). Jesus will make the world our perfect home again. As we come, the Father, Himself, will meet us, embrace us, and we will be brought into the feast where there will not be strangers.

It is interesting to note that the earthly ministry of Jesus started with a feast at Canaan of Galilee, where He turned water into wine in the Gospel of John 2. He came to bring joy; the Lord of the feast, He endured scars of the legal verdict "not guilty" for us so we are no longer liable for our wrongdoings, but free to partake of the party and joy. Jesus' salvation is a feast when we believe in, and rest in, His work for us; He became real in our hearts.

The Prodigal Son story is another of God's home-going analogies. The son went on his way, being deceived by his mind that there were things outside of home that were fascinating, enjoyable, and better. At the end of his adventure, he realized that there wasn't any place better than home. God permitted every situation—famine, loneliness, degradation—to turn him back home. As he was approaching home, he was met with the waiting arms of his father. Immediately when he arrived, the celebration was set in motion. His older brother, who was not excited at first, had no good reason not to join in the celebration because this is the utmost feast that all of God's children will come to. Those that have lingered around the house, without the enjoyment of being at home, will eventually come to the celebration. Those that once strayed away will come back for the feast also.

Isaac Watts, an English hymn writer, and Theologian of the seventeen hundred speaks of it like this: "The will of Zion yields a thousand sacred sweets before we reach the heavenly fields or walk the garden street. We are marching through Immanuel's ground to fairer worlds on high. The strife is over; the battle done. Now the victor's triumph won. O let the song of praise be sung, Alleluia!"

Death's mightiest powers have done their worst, and Jesus has his fees dispersed. Let shouts of praise and joy burst. Alleluya!

Let us rejoice; the fight is won and darkness is conquered. Death undone, life triumphant! Alleluya. So age-to-age, each nation grows more like the heart of him who rose.

Joy comes again! All shall be well, friends serve now in heaven shall dwell; be reunited! Alleluya! The end of all our ways is love, Then rise with him to things above.

Jesus' death tells of joy beyond the grave. All mankind is noble through thee.

Rejoice and be glad! He loves who was slain; Christ in the world is beginning His reign

The kingdom is coming on earth as in heaven.

Rejoice and be glad for He dwells on this earth

On earth, as is heaven; His splendor is owned.

Divine Fellowship

1 John 1:7

How can the eternal God and His creation have fellowship, a mutual sharing or exchange? In fellowshipping with God, especially in prayer, that exchange will take place. You exchange your weakness for His strength and wisdom. Spending time in the Word and in prayer will bring confidence and love for God. The more time you spend in fellowship with Him, the more you know about His goodness and righteousness. The more fellowship you have in Him, the more you are convinced of your right as a joint heir with Jesus Christ

This place, in its current state, is not our final home. The Jews in exile had the same sentiment, as expressed in Psalm 137:1-4:

"By the rivers of Babylon, there we sat down yea, we wept when we remembered Zion

v.4 How shall we sing the Lord's song in a foreign land?"

There is a pull toward the home.

Different songs allude to the missing of our home. For example:

"God be with you until we meet again."

By His counsels' guide, uphold you,

With His sheep securely fold you,"

This was a song of farewell written by J.E. Rankinl to a departing friend, which could also be for our departure from this world until the day of resurrection.

Another of such songs written by C.F. Gellert is:

"Jesus lives; the terrors now can't.

O death, no more impale us. Jesus lives!

By this, we know thou, O grave canst not enthrall us, Alleluya!"

"Jesus lives to Him, though over all the world is given.

May we go when He is gone, rest and reign with Him in heaven."

With these kinds of songs and many more in different hymns, believers are encouraged to be steadfast because there will a time of reunion where there will be no more parting.

In Hebrews 10:23, the writer says, "Let us hold fast the confession of our hope without wavering, for He who promised faithful." We should hold fast to our confession and to the end, because He who has promised to take us back home is faithful. We can trust Him also, because He is our High Priest who has passed to the heavens, Jesus Christ the Son of God.

I know whom I believe and am persuaded to see that He is able to keep what I have committed to Him until that day (2 Tim. 1:12).

Psalm 107:43: "Whosesoever is wise will observe these things and they will understand the loving-kindness of the Lord!"

Notes and References

1. *Frederick K. C. Price (2002). Holy Spirit the Helper We All Need. Dr. Frederick K. C. Price Ministries*

2. *Frederick K.C. Price (1980). How to Obtain Strong Faith. Faith One Pub*

3. *Kenneth E. Hagin (1997). The Healing Anointing Faith Library Publications*

4. *Timothy Keller (2008). The Prodigal God. Penguin Group. Pp 22-24; 102-104*

5. *E. W. Kenyon & Don Gossett (2003). Words that Move Mountains. Whitaker House. Pp 59, 64-65*

6. *Joseph Prince (2007). Destined to Reign. Harrison House Publishers*

7. *C. H. Spurgeon (2014). All of Grace. Barbour Books*

8. *Encyclopedia Americana, Intentional Edition. Scholastic Library Publishing Inc. Danbury, Connecticut (2004)*

9. *Phillip Keller ( ). A Shepherd's Look at Psalm 23*

10. *Max Lucado (2012). Grace. Thomas Nelson Publishers*

11. *Joseph Prince (2013). Spiritual Warfare. Thomas Nelson Publishers*

12. *Steve McVey (1995). Grace Walk. Harvest House Publishers*

13. *J. Ayodeji Adewuya (2004). Transformed by Grace. Cascade Books. Pg. 16-17*

14. *Songs of Praise. Percy Dearmer (editor), Williams R. Vaughan (editor), Martin Shaw (editor)*

15. *Joseph Henry Thayer, Thayer's Greek Lexicon Electric Database, copyright 2000, 2006.Ωs*

16. *The Online Bible Thayer's Greek Lexicon and Brown Driver & Briggs Hebrew Lexicon, Copyright 1993. Woodside Bible Fellowship, Ontario, Canada*

Scripture quotations in this book are taken from the New King James Version of the Bible.

Salvation Prayer

It is easy to receive the salvation that this gracious God provides. He makes it easy because He wants everyone to be saved and have eternal life. So, if you want this gift, all you need to do is believe His son Jesus in your heart and confess Him with your mouth as you offer this prayer.

Dear God, I come to you confessing the Lord Jesus, and I believe that you raised Him from the dead for my justification. Thank you for the precious blood that He shed to wash away my sin. Because of His finished work, I am now your child and you are my Father. Thank you for giving me eternal life in Jesus name. Amen

How to get in touch with the author?
Email: olayelelaw@yahoo.com